GREAT EXPLORATIONS

HENRY HUDSON

In Search of the Northwest Passage

Steven Otfinoski

Marshall Cavendish
Benchmark
New York

Marshall Cavendish Benchmark
99 White Plains Road
Tarrytown, NY 10591-9001
www.marshallcavendish.us

All Internet sites were available and accurate when the book was sent to press.

Library of Congress Cataloging-in-Publication Data

Otfinoski, Steven.
Henry Hudson : in search of the Northwest Passage / by Steven Otfinoski.
p. cm.—(Great explorations)
Summary: An examination of the life and accomplishments of the famed
explorer who lent his name to several geographic locations in North
America—Provided by publisher.
Includes bibliographical references and index.
ISBN-13: 978-0-7614-2225-9
ISBN-10: 0-7614-2225-0
1. Hudson, Henry, d. 1611—Travel—Juvenile literature.
2. America—Discovery and exploration—English—Juvenile literature.
3. Explorers—America—Biography—Juvenile literature. 4. Explorers—Great
Britain—Biography—Juvenile literature. I. Title. II. Series.

E129.H8O86 2007
910'.92—dc22

2005027927

Photo research by Anne Burns Images

Cover photo and inset: North Wind Picture Archives

The photographs in this book are used by permission and through the courtesy of: *The Granger Collection:* 5, 33,
35, 60, 63. *The Image Works:* 7, 21, 29. *North Wind Picture Archives:* 9, 18, 22, 27, 30, 36, 40, 50, 52, 55, 70, 72.
Bridgeman Art Library: Private Collection/Christie's Images, 11; Private Collection/Archives Charmet, 25; Private
Collection/Stapleton Collection, 49, 53; Chateau Musee/Giraudon, 56. *Corbis:* Bettmann, 13, 15, 37, 43, 67;
Kelly-Mooney Photography, 41; Gianni Dagli Orti, 47. *Art Resource:* Tate Gallery, London, 64.

Printed in China
1   3   5   6   4   2

Contents

foreword

Few Europeans were more instrumental in opening North America to settlement than the English explorer Henry Hudson. Sailing at different times for his native England as well as for the Netherlands, Hudson helped give both countries strong footholds in North America.

While many explorers have one major waterway named in their honor, Hudson has three—the Hudson River, Hudson Bay, and Hudson Strait—all of which he was among the first to explore.

One of the last of the era known as the golden age of exploration, Hudson pursued his search for a northern passage to the East with courage and determination. For all his ability, however, Hudson had his weaknesses as well. He was inept at handling his crews and was a poor judge of character. Although he had a great knowledge of the sea and navigation, he had little insight into the hearts and minds

Henry Hudson c 1560 - 1611

7 1p/2

The steely determination that made Henry Hudson a fearless explorer is captured in this portrait on a British postage stamp.

of the men who served under him. That fault would eventually lead to the downfall of this great explorer. Here is his story.

O N E

The Missing Years

There are sizable gaps in the life stories of many early European explorers. Few of these adventurers remain as much a mystery as Henry Hudson. Little, if anything, is known about Hudson's first thirty-five years. The explorer seems to have suddenly appeared on the stage of history at the time of his first voyage of discovery in 1607.

Yet, using some good detective work, historians have been able to piece together a convincing picture of what Hudson's life might have been like before that fateful year.

The Hudson family was a respected one in London in the 1550s. Another Henry Hudson, probably Henry's grandfather, was a London alderman (or councilman) and one of the founders of the Muscovy Company, a private trading firm. Such companies sprang up in England and in other countries to trade with distant and newly discovered lands. The Muscovy Company sent ships to Russia to trade English wool for

This statue in Clinton Park, in Kingston, New York, is just one of the numerous memorials to Henry Hudson.

furs and gold. Russia was then called Muscovy, hence the company's name.

Henry Hudson was probably born in the early 1570s. Historians believe that his father was also an alderman and a property owner with substantial holdings. The explorer's father died of a fever in the 1560s, leaving eight sons and a wife. His widow, according to public records, remarried. Her new husband, Richard Champion, was elected lord mayor of London in 1566.

Many of Hudson's brothers and other relatives worked for the Muscovy Company in various capacities. Henry probably started out as a cabin boy on merchant ships or served at a trading outpost. He was taught how to sail and navigate at sea, and on land he learned the trading business and a foreign language. The young man gradually worked his way up to sailor and eventually to ship's captain.

There is evidence that Hudson may have sailed with English explorer John Davis on his third voyage in 1587. Davis's goal was to find a quicker sea route to Cathay, the ancient name for China, by sailing northwest across the Atlantic Ocean. China and the rest of the East had spices, silk, porcelain, and other goods increasingly desired by Europeans. For centuries these highly prized items had reached western Europe by means of a land route dominated by Arab traders. A sea route to Asia would allow Europeans to trade directly and more cheaply with the Chinese.

A Portuguese explorer, Vasco da Gama, had reached India in 1498 by sailing southeast around Africa and into the Indian Ocean. But this was a long and dangerous route. The English and other Europeans thought they could reach the East more quickly by sailing northeast or northwest.

Davis sailed farther north than any previously known explorer and entered a treacherous body of water filled with ice and whirlpools. He named this entryway the Furious Overfall. He was prevented from crossing its waters by floating sheets of ice called floes. Davis was convinced that the Furious Overfall was the Northwest Passage, the long-sought gateway to the Pacific Ocean and to Asia beyond.

Davis wrote two books about his expeditions in the mid-1590s. Although Hudson may or may not have sailed with him, it is very likely that Hudson read at least one of Davis's accounts of his voyages.

Soon it would be Hudson's turn to lead an expedition. By 1606 he had become an experienced sea captain and navigator. With a wife, Katherine, and three sons—Oliver, John, and Richard—he was ready to make a name for himself on his own voyage in search of a sea route to China.

Spices like the ones pictured here were among the most treasured goods that Western traders sought from the East.

John Davis

One of the leading navigators of the late 1500s, John Davis was born in Sandridge, England, about 1550. Beginning in 1585, he made three voyages to find the Northwest Passage through Canada to the Pacific. On his first expedition, he discovered Davis Strait, which flows between Greenland and Canada. On his next two voyages he explored Baffin Island and the western coast of Greenland. The passage he sought, however, eluded him.

Davis later sailed with other explorers. With Thomas Cavendish he sought a passage to Asia through the Strait of Magellan at the tip of South America. Although he failed to find the passage, he and his crew were the first Europeans to sight the Falkland Islands off South America's southeastern coast in 1592. In 1596 and 1597 he sailed with Sir Walter Raleigh to the Azores, a group of islands in the North Atlantic west of Portugal.

Between 1598 and 1605, Davis made three voyages to the East Indies in Southeast Asia. On his last voyage, his ship was attacked by pirates off the coast of Sumatra, and he was killed.

Davis was also an inventor. His Davis quadrant, a navigational tool, was used by generations of sailors and explorers.

This dashing Englishman is believed to be Thomas Cavendish, an explorer who sailed with John Davis in search of a route around South America to the East.

T W O

A Bold Plan

The Muscovy Company's trade with Russia was limited because the waterways it used to reach the nation froze in winter. The company's leaders wanted instead to trade with China and believed they might be able to reach it by finding a sea passage around Russia to the northeast.

In 1606 Henry Hudson presented the Muscovy Company with a new and daring plan for reaching eastern Asia. He proposed sailing directly north over the North Pole. This was a far shorter route than sailing northwest, as John Davis had done.

The directors of the Muscovy Company were impressed by Hudson's proposal and the support it received from such respected geographic experts as the Reverend Richard Hakluyt. Hakluyt recommended Hudson as "an experienced seaman" who "has in his possession secret information that will enable him to find the northeast passage."

Hudson's plan, however, was not originally his own. Robert Thorne,

In forming his bold plan, Hudson visited Richard Hakluyt's house in Bristol and studied charts in the reverend's library.

THE NORTH POLE

It may strike us as odd today that the geographers of Hudson's day thought the North Pole a region of sun and warmth, but to them it made perfect sense. Because of its location at the top of the world, they rightly reasoned that it received sunlight twenty-four hours per day. Their error was in assuming that all this sunlight would melt the polar ice cap and create warm, open waters. Today we know that the sun is actually farther away from the North Pole than anywhere else on Earth, and thus the region retains a frigid arctic climate.

Henry Hudson never got closer than about 600 miles (966 kilometers) to the North Pole before his ships were driven back by ice floes and freezing temperatures. While later explorers traveled closer to the pole, no human reached it until American Robert E. Peary and his African-American assistant, Matthew Henson, in 1909. Admiral Richard E. Byrd and aviator Floyd Bennett became the first people to cross the pole in an airplane in 1926.

African-American explorer Matthew Henson accompanied Robert E. Peary to the North Pole about three hundred years after Hudson attempted to reach the same elusive place.

who had sailed with Italian explorer John Cabot for the English in 1497, had written a pamphlet called "Thorne's Plan" in 1526. In it, Thorne proposed reaching the East by crossing the pole in a northeast or northwest direction. Thorne and later English geographers mistakenly believed the North Pole to be surrounded by warm and hospitable waters.

The Muscovy Company hired Hudson to find a route over the North Pole. They paid him 130 pounds, the English monetary unit, and gave him a small square-rigged, three-masted ship, the *Hopewell*. Because the expedition was headed for unknown waters, most reputable seamen would not sign on. Hudson and his experienced first mate, William Collins, were forced to hire men of questionable character, who were willing to risk their lives on a potentially dangerous voyage. The recruits included drunkards, troublemakers, and petty criminals. Hudson also brought along his middle son, John, as cabin boy.

On April 23, 1607, the *Hopewell*, with a crew of twelve, set sail from London down the Thames River to the open sea at Gravesend. Bad weather delayed their departure from Gravesend until May 1.

T H R E E

To the Top of the World

Although the Muscovy Company employed Hudson, he was not what we would today call a "company man." He had a fiercely independent spirit. The company directors had given him specific orders to sail northeast in pursuit of the North Pole. They preferred the islands and territories of the northeast, well charted by earlier explorers and traders, to the unknown regions of the northwest. But Hudson ignored their orders. Upon arriving at the Shetland Islands northeast of England on May 26, 1607, he sailed northwest instead.

Why northwest? No one knows for certain. It is possible that he was trying to find the Furious Overfall, which John Davis believed to be the gateway to the Northwest Passage.

As the *Hopewell* proceeded north, the weather grew colder and conditions harsher. The crew became increasingly restless. When the needle on the ship's compass appeared to go off course, the superstitious sailors

The stark beauty and immense size of Greenland are captured
in this engraving.

claimed the ship was doomed. Hudson managed to calm their fears and avert a mutiny.

On June 13, the crew sighted the eastern coast of Greenland, a vast island lying mostly above the Arctic Circle. It was then called Kalaallit Nunaat, and Hudson may have first seen it twenty years earlier while sailing with John Davis. The writer of Hudson's ship log at the time described Greenland as a "very high land for the most part covered in snow, the remaining part bare."

For two weeks the *Hopewell* followed the coast, with Hudson mapping the unexplored regions. As the ship progressed north, the weather turned increasingly bitter. The rigging froze and the sails stiffened, making them difficult for the crew to handle. Ice formed on the ropes, cutting and chafing the men's hands. Rain froze on the deck, making their labors all the more treacherous. Cold arctic waves rocked the ship day and night. Thick fog developed, so the crew members could not see where they were going. Ice floes began to appear regularly in the frigid waters. The crew was afraid they would ram one and the ship would sink.

Soon the ice became a solid mass in the water, making progress impossible. Hudson reluctantly changed direction, steering for the northeast, his original course. On June 21, the *Hopewell* steered a course toward Newland, a chain of rugged islands first discovered by the Dutch in 1596. Today they are called Spitsbergen. Within a week, the expedition reached the shores of West Spitsbergen Island.

The crew gazed in amazement at the numerous seals and walruses sunning on the rocks off the island's coast. By mid-July, the *Hopewell* reached the northernmost island and entered a vast sheltered bay. Pods, or groups, of whales swam around them, at times brushing up against the ship. Hudson named it Whale's Bay and, with some of the crew, went ashore to explore the island. The warm climate and thriving wildlife raised Hudson's hopes that the North Pole, still almost 600 miles (966 kilometers) away, would be equally hospitable.

Greenland—Island of Ice

When Hudson sighted Greenland, it had already been explored and settled for more than six centuries. Viking explorer Eric the Red first sailed there in 982. The colony he established flourished and eventually grew to three thousand people. For more than four hundred years the Greenland colony thrived on the southeastern coast, the mildest corner of this mostly ice-covered land. For a time Greenland was a part of Norway. Then in 1380 it became a colony of Denmark.

By the fifteenth century, the European colony had died out from increasingly cold weather and the attacks of hostile Inuit, a native northern people. It was not until more than a century after Hudson had passed Greenland's coastal waters that Europeans again set up permanent communities on the island. Norwegian missionary Hans Egede established a settlement there in 1721. Denmark continued to govern Greenland, granting it control of its internal affairs in 1979. Today 90 percent of Greenlanders are of mixed Inuit and Danish descent. The world's largest island remains one of the least populated and most desolate places on Earth.

Viking explorer Erik the Red, shown here, was the discoverer of Greenland. His son, Leif Ericsson, supposedly sailed across the Atlantic Ocean to become the first European discoverer of North America.

Walruses were not an uncommon sight in the arctic waters
that Hudson sailed on his first two voyages.

As the ship continued north, the ice floes returned and gradually
became a solid, impenetrable barrier. Before Hudson knew it, the
Hopewell was surrounded by ice, unable to move. Desperately, the crew
tried to push the ice away with poles and their bare hands. They even

attempted to tow the ship to open water with a shallop, a small boat used for reaching shore, but their efforts were in vain.

Finally, when all seemed lost, a powerful northwest wind pushed the ship free of the ice and into open water. "May God give us thankful hearts for so great deliverance," Hudson wrote in his journal.

By the end of July, Hudson knew any further attempt to reach the polar region would be dangerous and foolhardy. To the crew's great relief, he gave the order to return home.

The *Hopewell* arrived in England on September 15, 1607, having been gone for three and a half months. Henry Hudson had sailed farther north than anyone before him. But he saw his expedition as a dismal failure. He was not, however, about to give up his search for a sea passage to the East.

F O U R

Back to the Arctic

Although Henry Hudson did not find passage to the East by crossing the North Pole, he had discovered something that pleased the Muscovy Company almost as much. His report of whales in Spitsbergen led the company to organize an expedition to the region to hunt them. The directors asked Hudson to lead the expedition, but he was not interested. He wanted to continue his search for a northern route to Asia. So a grateful Muscovy Company agreed to finance a second expedition.

Hudson had hoped for a larger, sturdier ship for his second voyage, but the directors assigned him to the *Hopewell* again. The explorer made the best of the situation and prepared thoroughly for the rough arctic waters. He had the ship's hull strengthened with wooden planks that could stand up to the hulking, jagged ice floes. He replaced the mainmast with a thicker one and bought a bigger and stronger shallop for sending exploration parties ashore. He increased the supply of

EARLY WHALING

Henry Hudson's discovery of the whales at Spitsbergen gave rise to the English whaling industry. Humans had hunted whales as far back as four thousand years ago. The Basque people of northern Spain and southern France established the first large-scale whaling industry in the Bay of Biscay in the tenth century.

Whales were principally hunted not for their meat but for their blubber or fat. Whale blubber was cooked to make oil, which for centuries was used as fuel in lamps. Whale bones and baleen, the thin plates hanging from the upper jaw of baleen whales, were also used to make dress hoops, whips, women's corsets, and other products in the eighteenth and nineteenth centuries.

Over a period of two centuries, English whalers killed more than 100,000 whales at Spitsbergen. In the twentieth century, whaling was banned in most countries to save whales from extinction. Japan and Russia, however, continue to hunt whales despite international pressure to stop.

Hudson's discovery of whales at Spitsbergen led directly to the rise of the European whaling industry.

meat for the trip to better fortify the crew for the hardships ahead. Hudson also bought muskets and a small cannon in case they encountered hostile native peoples.

Hudson was less thorough when it came to picking his crew of fourteen. Only three had sailed on his first voyage. For some unexplained reason, he chose fifty-year-old Robert Juet, a mean-tempered man of questionable character, to serve as first mate. He may have been impressed by Juet's toughness and his experience at sea, but Juet would prove a bad choice for second in command.

Hudson showed better judgment in bringing aboard Philip Staffe, a skilled carpenter and a man of good character. Both Juet and Staffe would sail on all three of Hudson's remaining voyages. Once again John Hudson served as cabin boy.

Hudson had a somewhat clearer idea of his route this time and was willing to try and find a passage to the northeast. He met and discussed the expedition with Hakluyt and other geographers, who agreed with him that the best passage to Asia lay to the northeast—above two large islands called Novaya Zemlya, off the northern coast of Russia.

The *Hopewell* set sail on April 22, 1608. In six weeks it reached the northern coast of Norway. From there Hudson set his course for Novaya Zemlya. By early June the ship was once more in ice-filled waters. On June 15, Hudson recorded that two members of the crew each sighted a mermaid, a mythical creature that is half human, half fish.

"She was close to the ship's side and looking earnestly at the men . . ." he wrote. "Her back and breasts were like a woman's, her body as big as ours, her skin very white, and she had long black hair hanging down behind."

In late June the ship reached Novaya Zemlya and was driven back by ice floes. Hudson failed to find a navigable channel between the two islands, but he did have his men explore the coasts. Crew members were happily surprised to find fields of green grass, wildflowers, and

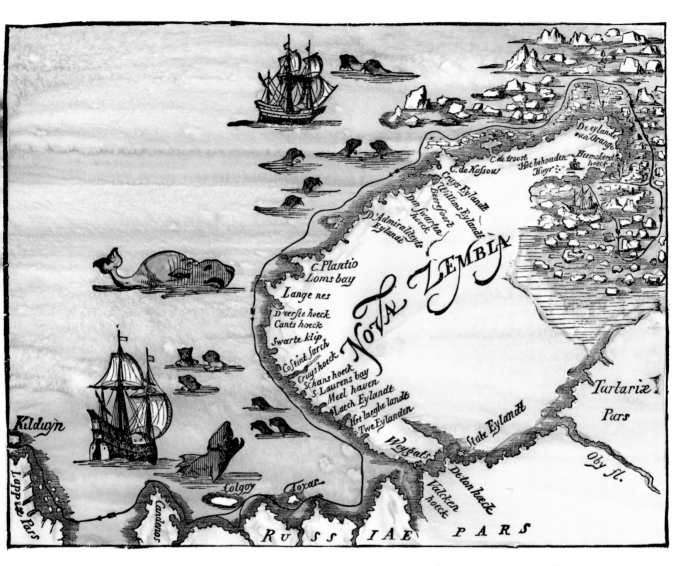

This map of "Nova Zembla," another name for Novaya Zemlya, is taken from a 1598 book on exploration. Note the great variety of sea life that the mapmaker included as illustration.

MERMAIDS—SIRENS OF THE SEA

When the two sailors on the *Hopewell* said they saw a mermaid, their mates believed them. Most sailors in Hudson's day believed in mermaids. The notion had existed for centuries.

Stories and legends about beautiful women with fish tails instead of legs have existed since prehistory. According to some legends, mermaids, with their beauty and enchanting songs, lured sailors to their death. Some mermaids were not so treacherous and actually fell in love with mortal men. These mermaids were even able to assume a complete human shape in order to marry the objects of their affection.

While mermaids may seem fanciful creatures to us today, there may be a scientific basis for the persistent belief in them. The sea cow, or manatee, is a sea mammal, the only one—other than whales—that lives its entire life in water. With a human-sized head and mammary glands, the female sea cow somewhat resembles a human in the water. A mistaken sighting may have given rise to the legend of the mermaid.

A mermaid comes face to face with a manatee in this
nineteenth-century wood engraving. The manatee, seen
from a distance, was often mistaken for a human,
giving rise to the mermaid legend.

Arctic ice floes were a constant threat to Hudson and his men
on the explorer's second voyage.

streams on Novaya Zemlya. They also found abundant wildlife, including ducks, geese, swans, deer, and walruses. They shot a number of the geese for food and collected birds' eggs to eat.

Hudson did not let this latest setback discourage him. He was not ready to give up on his goal. He followed one of the island's rivers north, but an iceberg soon blocked the way. He finally decided to turn back. The crew members thought they were returning home to England, but Hudson had other plans. He secretly set sail for the northwest, in search of the Furious Overfall.

It was unwise of him not to inform the crew of his plans, for when the men finally realized where they were headed, they were enraged. Juet, their spokesman, threatened to mutiny unless Hudson returned them to England. The captain had no choice but to agree. Under pressure, he agreed to write and sign a statement that declared he was returning to England of his own free will. That way, he could not later accuse the crew of attempted mutiny, which was an offense punished by hanging.

The *Hopewell* arrived in England on August 26, 1608. Hudson had made accurate maps of both Novaya Zemlya and the Great Ice Barrier, the edge of the ice shelf extending from Antarctica. They would prove extremely useful to geographers. The Muscovy Company, however, was not impressed. They wanted a route to the East, and Hudson had again failed to find it. When he proposed a third voyage, they refused to sponsor it.

The Reverend Samuel Purchas, a friend of Hudson's, described him a short time later as having "sunk into the lowest depths of the Humour [mental state] of Melancholy from which no man could rouse him."

To Henry Hudson, it must have seemed that his exploring career had come to an abrupt end. That notion was soon proved wrong.

FIVE

Sailing for the Dutch

In the autumn of 1608, Emanuel van Meteran, the Dutch consul in London, invited Henry Hudson to dinner. Van Meteran was also a representative of the Dutch East India Company (DEIC), a successful Eastern trading company. He suggested that the explorer consider an offer to sail for them. Shortly afterward, Hudson was invited to come to the Netherlands and meet with the company's directors. Convinced he would find no better offers to organize another expedition, he accepted.

The DEIC already had a thriving monopoly among the Dutch in the East. The company's ships followed the route the Portuguese had blazed years earlier—eastward around Africa's Cape of Good Hope. It was a long and arduous route. Some of the company's directors wanted Hudson to try again to find a shorter route to Asia by traveling over the North Pole. But other company officials were not sure the route was possible and stalled on making the Englishman an offer.

This nineteenth-century engraving shows Hudson signing a contract in January 1609 to lead an expedition for the Dutch East India Company.

Meanwhile, the French ambassador had met secretly with Hudson to see if the explorer was interested in sailing for France. When the Dutch got word of this meeting, they stopped the delaying and quickly made Hudson an offer in January 1609.

Their terms were less than generous. They offered Hudson a salary of 800 Dutch guilders, the equivalent of half of what the Muscovy Company had paid him for his first voyage. The ship they gave him, the *Half Moon*, was smaller and less seaworthy than the *Hopewell* and poorly equipped for such a long voyage. When Hudson insisted on a better ship, the directors flatly refused. They also insisted that half of Hudson's crew be Dutch, a decision that would later lead to many problems.

Perhaps having heard of Hudson's wandering ways on past voyages, the Dutch made him swear on a Bible that he would sail only in one direction to find a northern passage—"by the north around the

THE DUTCH EAST INDIA COMPANY

The Dutch East India Company was only seven years old when its directors hired Henry Hudson to find a new route to the East. It had been granted a charter to trade in the Far East by the Dutch government in 1602. The company's goals, set forth in the charter, were to expand and protect Dutch trade interests in the East and to prevent competition among Dutch trading companies. In return, the company was given a monopoly on Dutch trade from east of Africa to west of the Strait of Magellan in South America.

The DEIC established its headquarters at Batavia, now Jakarta, on the island of Java in 1619. The Dutch company soon drove the Portuguese and British traders out of the region and brought local native leaders under its control. The company prospered in the pepper and spice trade and enriched itself and the Netherlands. In 1652 the company established a Dutch colony at the Cape of Good Hope in present-day South Africa.

Corruption eventually cost the DEIC its wealth and reputation. Nearly bankrupt by the late eighteenth century, the Dutch government disbanded the company in 1799 and seized its holdings. It was an inglorious end to two centuries of success and prosperity.

A prosperous Dutch merchant in Batavia points to the
trading ships that are the source of much of his wealth in
this seventeenth-century painting.

north side of Nova Zembla [Novaya Zemlya]." If he found no passage, he was to return at once. It was an oath that Hudson had no intention of keeping.

Hudson's thoughts were again turning to the northwest. His friend John Smith, one of the founders of Jamestown (in present-day Virginia), the first permanent English settlement in North America, had written him a letter. Smith urged him to look for a waterway north of Jamestown that the local Indians had claimed led to the Pacific. Like many people of the time, Smith believed America was a narrow strip of land separating the Atlantic and the Pacific.

Among the English half of his crew, Hudson retained John

Hudson's ship the Half Moon sets sail from Amsterdam on its historic voyage to the New World.

Colman, who had sailed with him on his first voyage, and Robert Juet. In Hudson's mind, Juet's abilities as a navigator may have outweighed his liability as a troublemaker. Hudson's son John was again appointed cabin boy.

The *Half Moon* set sail from Amsterdam, Netherlands, on April 6, 1609. From the start, the voyage was plagued with problems. The English and Dutch sailors could not understand each other's languages and did not get along. "I hope that these square-faced men know the sea," John Colman wrote to his wife about the Dutch crew members.

Native Americans from present-day Maine are welcomed aboard the
Half Moon to trade furs and animal skins. Not all of Hudson's
meetings with Indians during the voyage would go so smoothly.

"Looking at their fat bellies, I fear they think more highly of eating than of sailing."

Colman's worst fears soon proved true. The Dutch sailors refused to work in the cold weather, which they were not used to. At the first sign of a storm, they would go belowdecks to eat pickled fish, their favorite food, while the resentful English seamen did all the work.

As the *Half Moon* approached the northern coast of Norway, the weather grew worse, and Hudson decided to change his course for the west and head for North America. This time, he laid his plans before the crew members, who were already turning mutinous, and promised them warmer weather and calmer waters if they agreed to sail westward. The crew accepted the plan, and the ship headed across the Atlantic.

It was a stormy crossing that took about a month. As July began, the *Half Moon* reached the Grand Banks of present-day Newfoundland on Canada's eastern coast. The group anchored in George's Harbor, Hudson's first landing in the New World, then proceeded south to Maine's Penobscot Bay. There the men went ashore to cut timber for a new mast. The old one had been damaged in a storm. On land, they had their first encounter with Native Americans. The native people were friendly and traded beaver skins and other furs for cloth, knives, and beads. The *Half Moon* then sailed farther south past Cape Cod in what is today known as Massachusetts, which Hudson named "New Holland."

By the middle of August, the *Half Moon* reached present-day Virginia. Remembering John Smith's story of a Northwest Passage, Hudson sailed his ship north again in search of it.

SIX

River of Mountains

As the *Half Moon* sailed north, Hudson paused to investigate two large bays—the Chesapeake Bay (in what are today Maryland and Virginia) and the Delaware Bay (in present-day Delaware and New Jersey). He encountered bad weather in the Chesapeake and shoals in the Delaware. Neither bay, Hudson concluded, was the Northwest Passage he was seeking. Oddly enough, Hudson did not attempt to sail from Chesapeake Bay up the James River to Jamestown to see his friend John Smith.

Then on September 2, 1609, the *Half Moon* entered a big harbor and the crew sighted Manhattan Island, which means "island of hills" in the Algonquian Indian language. Over the next few days, Hudson explored nearby Staten Island and New Jersey. What most interested the explorer, however, was the mouth of a river that flowed into New York Bay. When he questioned the local Lenape Indians about it, they indicated in sign language that the river was very wide. Hudson wondered if this could at last be the fabled passage that he was seeking.

On September 6, he sent John Colman and four other crew members to explore another river that flowed beside Manhattan Island. While paddling a canoe along a channel, the party was attacked by a band of Lenape. Colman was shot in the throat by an arrow and died instantly. Two other men were wounded.

The rest of the search party brought Colman's body back to the ship. Under Hudson's orders, he was buried at the very spot where he died. Hudson named it Colman's Point, which it is still called today. He readied the cannon and prepared the men for another Indian attack.

Canoes filled with Indians greet Hudson as he begins his celebrated voyage up the river that today bears his name.

Soon afterward, two canoes of armed Indians approached the ship to trade. The crew held two of the visitors hostage to discourage further attacks. On September 12, Hudson started up the river that the Indians called *Muhheakunnuk*, meaning "great waters constantly in motion." Hudson called it River of Mountains. Today it is called, in his honor, the Hudson River.

Henry Hudson was not the first European to sail up the Hudson

River. Italian explorer Giovanni da Verrazano, sailing for France, had come upon the waterway eighty-five years earlier. But Verrazano had been more interested in exploring the New England coast and had traveled only a short distance upriver.

Hudson and his men were awestruck by the imposing cliffs of the area that later became New Jersey's Palisades rising across from the lush green hills of Manhattan Island. As the sailors entered the Hudson River valley, they marveled at its abundant wildlife and rich vegetation. They were equally impressed by the Catskill Mountains, which bordered the

The New Jersey Palisades lining parts of the lower Hudson River have changed little since Hudson and his crew first saw them from the deck of their ship.

THE HUDSON RIVER

Henry Hudson probably had no idea how important the river later named in his honor would become one day. The Dutch settled Manhattan Island only fifteen years after Hudson's voyage. They also established settlements in the Hudson River valley. Later explorers would use the river to reach Canada. The first successful steamboat, built and operated by Robert Fulton in 1807, trudged up the Hudson on its maiden voyage.

Today the Hudson River remains one of the major trade waterways in the United States. Large ships can still travel to Albany, New York, as the *Half Moon* did. Smaller vessels can continue on another 6 miles (9.7 kilometers) to Troy.

Although pollution has muddied the pristine waters of the river for many years, a recent cleanup campaign has reversed much of the damage. People can swim and even fish in the Hudson, as they once did. Many parts of the river are as striking today as they were when Hudson and his crew first laid eyes on them.

winding river farther north. The land was, Hudson wrote in his journal, "the finest for cultivation that I ever in my life set foot upon."

As the river widened, he was convinced he had found the passage to the Pacific he had sought for so long. Near present-day West Point, the two Indian hostages escaped and swam to shore.

The crew was not greatly concerned: the Indians that they now encountered were friendlier and more peaceful than those downriver. They stopped at one Mohegan village where they were treated to a feast of pigeons, sweet corn, a mash made of tree parts, and a fat dog, which Hudson noted was "killed . . . and skinned . . . in great haste."

A day later, they reached what is today Albany, New York, where they dropped anchor and traded with the local Indians. To Hudson's disappointment, the river was growing narrower. He sent a small expedition party ahead in the shallop to investigate. They returned with the discouraging news that the river was only 7 feet (2 meters) deep

Hudson and his men are invited to a feast at a village along the river. While he responded well to Indians when they were friendly and welcoming, Hudson's attitude toward the region's native residents was indifferent at best.

24 miles (39 kilometers) ahead. Disappointed, Hudson gave the order to turn the ship around. They had traveled 150 miles (242 kilometers) from the river's mouth, about half of its entire length.

The return trip was largely uneventful until they reached Peekskill on October 1. They stopped to trade with the Indians, and one native man slipped into Juet's cabin and stole some clothing. A Dutch sailor caught him and shot him dead. A second Indian sneaked aboard from a canoe and was killed by the ship's cook. The other Indians fled.

Fearing reprisals from the Indians, Hudson sailed several miles downriver before stopping for the night. But news of the killings spread quickly, and the next day Indians attacked the ship as it neared Manhattan. The crew fired their guns at the Indians, killing as many as ten. Hudson did not want to risk another fight, and on October 4 the *Half Moon* sailed on through the night into the open waters of the Atlantic.

But Hudson was not through with North America. He wanted to winter in Newfoundland and in the spring head farther north. There he hoped to find the Furious Overfall, which seemed the most likely passage to the Orient. But the ship's supplies were low, and the men were anxious to be on their way home. Hudson feared he might have a mutiny on his hands if he tried to make his crew stay the winter.

So Hudson set his course for England and arrived at Dartmouth on November 7, 1609. Why Hudson landed first in England and not the Netherlands is something of a mystery. Some historians suggest he may have been working as a secret agent for the English while employed by the Dutch. If that were true, it would not explain the surprising reception he received once back in his homeland.

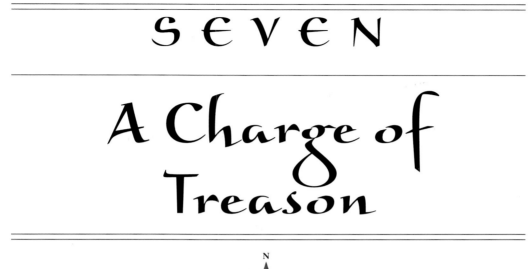

A Charge of Treason

Once back in England, Hudson wasted no time writing to the directors of the Dutch East India Company, describing his experiences and asking for more funds to refit the *Half Moon* and return to North America.

The directors told him to return with his ship to Amsterdam at once. But word of Hudson's voyage for the Dutch reached King James I of England who was furious that an English explorer would dare offer his services to another country. The discovery of the Northwest Passage would make the Dutch rich and shut England out of the profitable trade with the East.

Hudson was officially blamed for "voyaging to the detriment [harm] of his country" and was forbidden to leave England.

Hudson was then ordered to London to face charges of treason. While he awaited trial, he was placed under house arrest. The *Half Moon* remained in England and was not brought back to Amsterdam

King James I of England

It is not surprising that many important people opposed King James's treatment of Henry Hudson. They opposed nearly everything that the king did.

James was a somewhat haughty ruler who tried to restore the divine right of kings, a belief that monarchs derived their authority directly from God. This concept was no longer widely accepted in England by James's time. He also had the misfortune to succeed one of the most beloved monarchs of English history—his cousin Elizabeth I, who died in 1603. For much of his reign, James battled with the English Parliament in a struggle for power.

Despite his problems with Hudson, James was a patron of explorers and enthusiastically supported the exploration of North America. The first settlers of Virginia were so grateful to him that they named their settlement Jamestown in his honor. James played a more indirect role in the settlement of the second permanent English colony in America. His persecution of the Puritans, worshippers who wanted to reform the Church of England, forced them to leave England to find a new home in present-day Massachusetts.

James was also a great patron of the arts. He issued a royal license to playwright William Shakespeare and his company of actors, making them "the King's Men." With his support, a group of scholars also composed a new English version of the Bible, the celebrated King James Bible.

James was something of an author himself. Among his written works is a book about witches and witchcraft, on which he prided himself an expert, and an attack on the colonial crop that became the craze of London—tobacco.

King James I of England was often strong willed. His forceful thoughts and opinions sometimes set him at odds with both his advisors and subjects.

by Hudson's Dutch crew until July 1610. All of Hudson's charts and logbooks were also taken to Amsterdam, considered the property of the Dutch East India Company. Regrettably, this treasure trove of information on Hudson's historic third voyage was eventually lost, although some of Hudson's journals survive.

Despite King James's position, many Englishmen were sympathetic to Hudson's misfortune. Some came to visit him while he suffered under house arrest. Among them was an earnest young man named Henry Greene. Greene expressed his admiration of Hudson and raised his spirits at a time when they needed lifting.

Other men who supported Hudson were more powerful, important figures with strong connections. Sir Thomas Smythe, for one, was a founder and governor of the Virginia Company and the English East India Company (EIC).

The king was finally persuaded to withdraw the charges against Hudson. The explorer was a free man. Sir Thomas and several other prosperous men formed the Company of Gentlemen, a group that sponsored an expedition of discovery to be led by Hudson under the direction of the EIC. He eagerly accepted their offer.

The expedition would be more elaborate than any he had previously undertaken. The ship he would sail, the *Discovery*, was 65 feet (20 meters) long and larger and sturdier than either of his two previous ships. The company gave him enough money to buy sufficient supplies and hire a crew of twenty-two. Best of all, the Company of Gentlemen gave Hudson the freedom to chart his own course to North America, putting no restrictions on where his voyage might lead him.

Hudson's fortunes may have improved, but not his judgment of character. When it came time to pick the crew, most of the men he chose were from the lower levels of English society. Again Hudson hired the quarrelsome Robert Juet as his first mate. He also brought aboard Philip Staffe and his own son John. A new addition was

Sir Thomas Smythe was one of the powerful merchants who helped finance Hudson's fourth and final voyage.

A sturdy and well-equipped ship was an essential ingredient for a successful journey. This illustration appeared in Voyages, Hudson's journal of an early expedition published in 1612 after the explorer's death.

Abacuk Prickett, an employee of one of the sponsors, who was given the task of keeping a journal of the voyage.

The *Discovery* left London on April 17, 1610, and arrived at Gravesend five days later. During the ship's brief stay there, Hudson made one last change in personnel. He sent ashore a representative of the Company of Gentlemen and took on board Henry Greene as his replacement. Hudson may have thought the representative was sent to spy on him. As for Greene, Hudson liked him and saw him as someone whose loyalty and support he could count on during the long voyage they faced. That impression, along with many other things, would change in the fateful months ahead.

E I G H T

Troubled Waters

By May 11 the crew of the *Discovery* sighted Iceland. The men watched in awe as a volcano, Mount Hekla, erupted. Bad weather followed, and they were stranded off Iceland for two weeks. They passed the time as best they could, bathing in the island's hot springs and hunting the abundant fish and game birds. It would be one of the most pleasant phases of their trip, spoiled only by the outbreak of a fight. Henry Greene, who had previously been in trouble with the law for gambling, got into a disagreement with the ship's surgeon, Edward Wilson. Hudson thoughtlessly took Greene's side in the argument, a move that alienated the rest of the crew. Juet subsequently spread rumors that Greene was a spy for the captain, a charge that may have been true.

Hudson was furious with Juet for stirring up dissension among the crew. He threatened to throw him off the ship at the next island they passed, but others persuaded Hudson not to. The tense moments passed, but the crew's resentment continued to simmer under the surface.

The *Discovery* rounded Greenland and completed the icy North Atlantic crossing in several weeks. On June 25 it reached "the mountaynes of ice" that marked the mouth of the Furious Overfall, which Hudson had long sought. Today it is called Hudson Strait. The wide turbulent channel, which runs between Baffin Island to the north and present-day Labrador and Quebec to the south, posed new threats to the ship. Dangerous ice floes and thick, impenetrable fog made progress slow and the sailors especially cautious.

Days passed, and the fear of the unknown gripped the men as tightly as the freezing cold. They finally refused to go any farther. Confident that he had found his path to the Pacific at last, Hudson tried to calm the crew's fears by showing them his maps and charts. The crew reluctantly agreed to continue.

Three or four weeks and 450 miles (725 kilometers) later, the

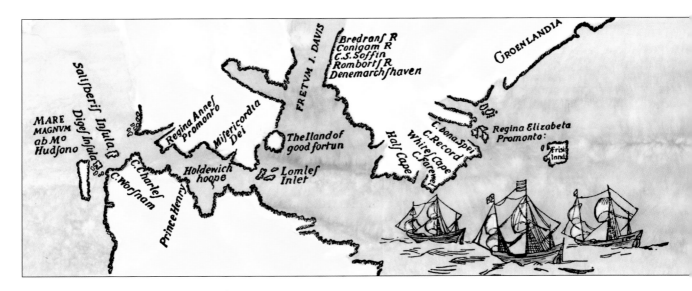

This map of one of Hudson's expeditions was published in 1612 in *Voyages*. At the time, many people believed the book had been written not by Hudson but by his son Oliver.

Hudson returned to the frozen regions of the far north for his fourth voyage.

Discovery entered an open body of water so vast that Hudson was convinced he had reached the Pacific Ocean. It was actually Hudson Bay. He set his course southward, believing he would soon glimpse the East. Eventually he entered another smaller body of water, what is today James Bay.

For several frustrating weeks, Hudson tried in vain to find a way out of James Bay. The crew's discontent again rose to a boil. They urged him to sail west in Hudson Bay, figuring this would lead to the East, but he would not listen. Juet tried to organize a mutiny.

On September 10, Hudson put Juet on trial for disloyalty. The testimony of other crew members—some of them disliked Juet as much as Hudson did—showed Juet to be disloyal, and he was found guilty. Hudson demoted him to common seaman and made Robert Bylot first mate. Juet's resentment was further fueled by the possibility that he might be charged with mutiny back in England and hanged. He had become a man with little to lose.

Hudson continued to doggedly explore every corner of James Bay for a channel leading south. By late October, the *Discovery* was trapped on all sides by ice floes and unable to move. Hudson anchored the ship

HUDSON BAY—CANADA'S INLAND SEA

It is not surprising that Henry Hudson mistook Hudson Bay for the Pacific Ocean. Approximately 316,500 square miles (819,735 square kilometers) in size, it is more than three times the area of all the Great Lakes combined. The landmasses that surround it give it the appearance of a vast inland sea.

Today, Hudson Bay remains almost as wild and remote as it was when Hudson first saw it. The only commercial activity on its waters is shipping, and that is limited to just three months each year when the bay is free of ice. The principal residents on the shores surrounding the bay are Native Americans, and most work is in trade or construction.

The Hudson Bay Railway—built in 1929—runs from Churchill, Manitoba, on the western shore of the bay, to the western Canadian provinces. A group of hydroelectric stations was built on the La Grande River at James Bay in 1971 to supply power to the region.

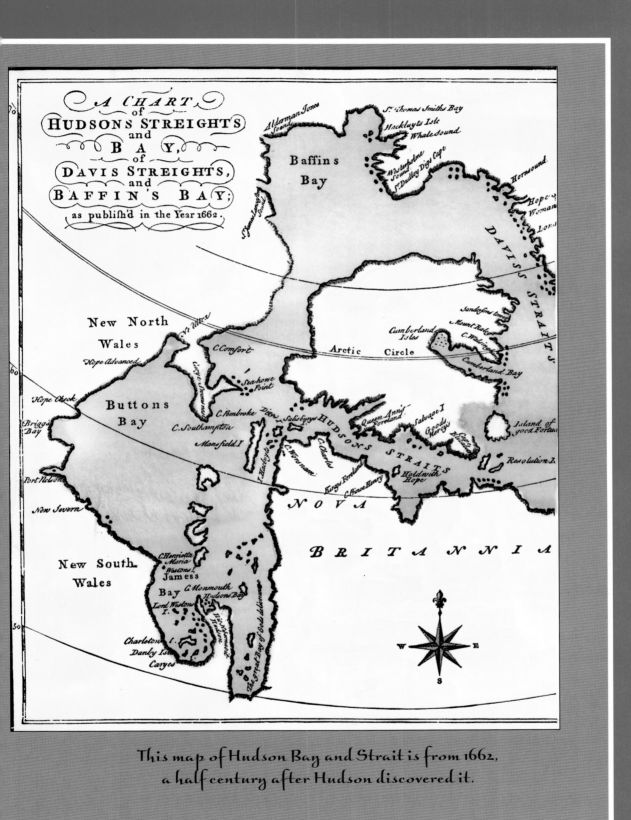

A CHART
of
HUDSONS STREIGHTS
and
BAY,
of
DAVIS STREIGHTS,
and
BAFFIN'S BAY;
as publish'd in the Year 1662.

Baffins Bay

New North Wales

New South Wales

Buttons Bay

Jamess Bay

Arctic Circle

NOVA

BRITANNIA

HUDSONS STRAITS

DAVIS STRAITS

This map of Hudson Bay and Strait is from 1662,
a half century after Hudson discovered it.

It was harsh conditions like these that led Hudson's men
to fear for their lives and resent their leader's refusal
to turn around and head home.

near the mouth of the Nottaway River around November 1 and sent a
party ashore to find game to restock their dwindling food supplies.

One crew member, John Williams, wandered off by himself and
became lost in the forest. They later found him frozen to death. It was
the custom when a man died on a long voyage to auction off his clothing. With a frigid winter ahead of them, everyone wanted a chance to
bid for Williams's warm woolen coat. But the captain agreed to sell the

Of Hudson's four voyages, the last two turned out to have a major
impact on the colonization and settling of North America.

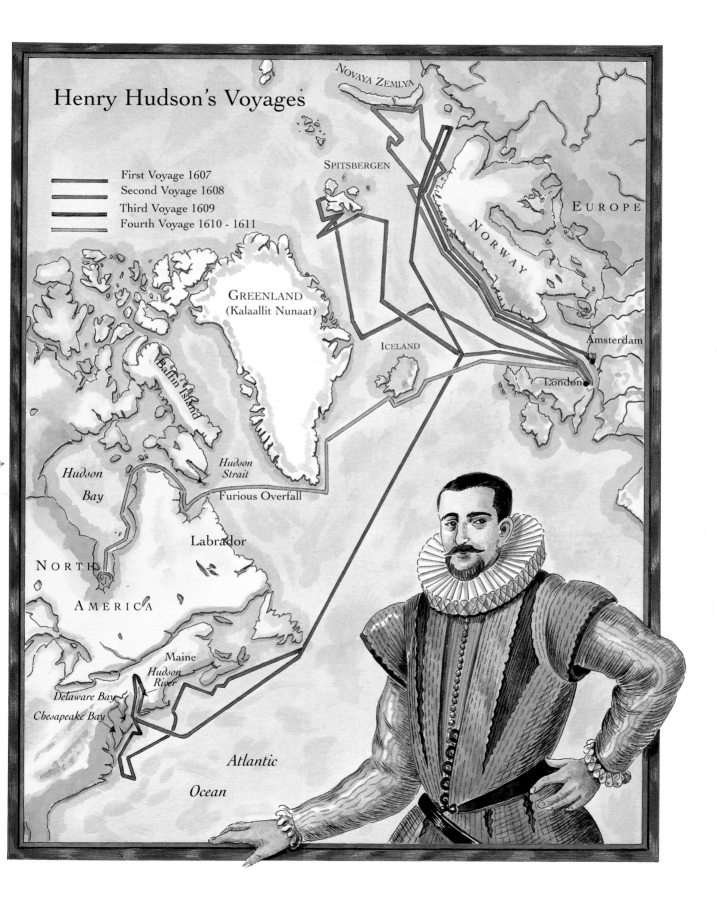

Henry Hudson's Voyages

First Voyage 1607
Second Voyage 1608
Third Voyage 1609
Fourth Voyage 1610 - 1611

NOVAYA ZEMLYA

SPITSBERGEN

EUROPE

NORWAY

GREENLAND
(Kalaallit Nunaat)

ICELAND

Amsterdam

London

Baffin Island

Hudson
Bay

Hudson
Strait

Furious Overfall

Labrador

NORTH

AMERICA

Maine

Hudson
River

Delaware Bay

Chesapeake Bay

Atlantic

Ocean

coat to Greene. Such favoritism inflamed the crew. Perhaps realizing his mistake, Hudson tried to appease them by ordering Staffe, the ship's carpenter, to build a shelter on shore with some extra wood they had onboard. Staffe refused, stating rightly that Hudson had waited too late in the season for such a project and that it was too cold to build on land.

Hudson then foolishly lashed out at one of his most loyal supporters and threatened to hang Staffe for insubordination. "The house," Prickett wrote in his journal, "was finally made, with much labor, but of little use."

Soon afterward, Staffe went hunting onshore with Greene. Hudson was furious with Greene for befriending Staffe and sold Williams's coat to Bylot instead. He then reminded Greene that he was not a regular member of the crew and might not be paid his wages if he misbehaved. From that moment on, Henry Greene—once Hudson's faithful friend—became one of his worst enemies.

As winter continued, the food supplies started to shrink, and the once plentiful game disappeared from the frozen land. "We went . . . in search of anything that had any substance to it, no matter how vile," wrote Abacuk Prickett. "Nothing was spared, including moss of the ground, compared to which rotten wood is better. . . ."

Sick, cold, and resentful of their unyielding captain, the crew of the *Discovery* hunkered down and waited for spring when the ice would thaw and they would be freed from their frigid prison.

N I N E

Mutiny!

By mid-June 1611, the spring sun had melted the ice on James Bay. After eight months of deprivation and cold, the *Discovery* was finally free to continue its journey, but the tensions between Henry Hudson and a large portion of his crew did not dissolve as well. Most of the crew had little confidence that their captain could find a way out of the bay, much less get them back to England. When Hudson ordered the men's sea chests broken open to search for hoarded food supplies, William Wilson and Henry Greene began to secretly plot a mutiny. Abacuk Prickett tried to stop the mutiny, but his objections had no effect.

On the morning of June 22 or 24, while the ship was anchored near the southern end of James Bay, the mutineers seized an unsuspecting Hudson as he left his cabin and tied him hand and foot.

The mutineers went about their work with ruthless speed. They loaded Hudson into the shallop, rounded up those crew members still

The mutiny onboard the Discovery, when it finally occurred,
was brief, brutal, and merciless.

loyal to the captain, as well as the weak and sick, and put them into the small boat with him. Among the captives was Hudson's son John. Philip Staffe volunteered to join Hudson in the boat. The mutineers did not want to lose Staffe—his woodworking skills would be a valuable asset on the voyage ahead. But the stalwart carpenter refused to stay aboard. At first the mutineers provided Hudson with no food or other necessities, but when Staffe demanded his carpenter's tools, they gave them to him. Perhaps out of guilt and shame, they also put a pot of grain and a gun and the shot and powder needed to fire it into the boat.

Then they towed the shallop behind the ship as it headed north. Hudson told Prickett, while he was still in earshot, to beware of Juet. Prickett replied that it was Greene who had led the mutiny. The words might well have stung Hudson more than the cold sea wind. Soon afterward, the mutineers cut the towrope, and the shallop faded into the distance as the ship sped ahead. That was the last the *Discovery* or anyone else ever saw of Hudson and his seven luckless companions.

Without Hudson to navigate the ship, the mutineers soon found themselves lost in the vast waters of Hudson Bay. They ransacked the remaining food supplies, which were soon gone. Exhausted and hungry, they reached Digge's Island on July 25. Greene and Wilson led a small party ashore to trade goods with the Inuit for food.

The Indians were friendly at first and even showed the men how to catch birds in traps. But the following day they launched a surprise attack. Wilson and Greene and two others were seriously wounded in the frantic struggle. Greene died of his wounds. The others managed to return to the ship, but soon afterward all three died of their injuries. With the two ringleaders gone, Robert Bylot took over as captain and proved a more capable leader than either Greene or Wilson.

Soon the *Discovery* was out of Hudson Bay and slowly making its way through Hudson Strait. Supplies of food again ran low, and the crew was reduced to eating the few seagulls they could catch. After they

THE HIGH CRIME OF MUTINY

Mutiny, in the seventeenth century, was one of the most serious crimes on the high seas. The mutineers of the *Discovery* must have been desperate men, because they knew if they were caught and convicted, they would likely end up hanging from the end of a rope.

Some mutineers had more justification for their violent acts than the crew of the *Discovery.* On the ships of Great Britain and other nations, life was hard and discipline extremely harsh. Perhaps the most famous mutiny in English history took place aboard the HMS *Bounty* in 1789. The story of the mutiny against the tyrannical Captain William Bligh and its aftermath was fictionalized in a trilogy of popular novels by Charles Nordhoff and James Norman Hall in the 1930s. Fletcher Christian, the leader of the mutiny, and eight other mutineers settled on Pitcairn Island in the South Pacific, with their Polynesian wives. Their descendants live there still.

ate the meat, they fried the gulls' bones in candle wax and ate them sprinkled with vinegar. In early August, Juet collapsed from starvation and died. With what little energy the remaining men had left, they threw his body overboard.

The eight survivors clung to life but were unable to do much else.

Henry Hudson gazes for the last time on the ship he once commanded. Several of the crew members who joined him were sick and weak, as is revealed in this painting.

The ship, meanwhile, lumbered across the North Atlantic in utter disrepair. Then on September 6, 1611, the reduced crew sighted the seacoast of Ireland. The *Discovery* finally reached London on October 20. The survivors were interrogated by the directors of the trading company, who recommended that they be hanged for mutiny. Surprisingly, their trial did not take place for another seven years. By that time half of them had died, and the four surviving defendants were all found not guilty and freed.

In a time when mutiny was a capital crime, how did these men

John Collier's painting The Last Voyage of Henry Hudson
shows a resigned Hudson facing certain death as he half heartedly
tries to comfort his young son.

escape punishment? There are at least two reasons. With all the ring-leaders dead, the defendants were able to place most of the blame on them. The men also incorrectly claimed to have discovered with Hudson the Northwest Passage. If they were hanged, that secret would die with them. So the officials opted for lenience. Both Bylot and Prickett eventually returned to North America on other expeditions.

And what of Henry Hudson and his small band of followers? What became of them? Several ships sailed from England to find Hudson and further explore the region over the next few years. But they found no sign of the castaways. Historians have offered several theories about their fates.

Some believe that they soon died at sea of hunger and exposure.

Others say that, under Hudson's command, the small party reached the shore and set up camp. Some years later, fur trappers came upon the ruins of a building on the shore of Hudson Bay. Was it built by Philip Staffe as a shelter for the castaways? Another crude structure was discovered in 1631 by an English captain on Danby Island in the bay. Even with a shelter, it is unlikely the group could have survived for long. They may even have been attacked by Inuit and killed.

A third theory claims that the Inuit befriended Hudson's party and adopted them into their tribe. Based on Hudson's generally indifferent treatment of Indians, this seems unlikely. However, two legends persist among the northern tribes that may support this theory. According to one legend, the Inuit found the floating shallop full of dead men and a boy who was still alive. They took him back to their village and supposedly tied him up with their dogs. Could this have been John Hudson, the explorer's son? The other legend states that Henry Hudson and his men were captured by the Inuit, enslaved, and later killed.

The facts of exactly what happened to Hudson and his unfortunate band will probably never be known. Still his accomplishments continue to shine forth out of the dark clouds surrounding the end of his life.

THE CATSKILL LEGEND OF HENRY HUDSON

Perhaps the most outlandish story of Henry Hudson's fate was conjured up by American author Washington Irving, who put the explorer into his most popular story, "Rip Van Winkle." In this American classic, Rip goes hunting with his dog in the Catskill Mountains and comes upon the ghosts of Hudson and his crew on the *Half Moon*. Irving depicts them as strange ghostly dwarfs, fond of drinking and bowling. They get poor Rip drunk, and he falls asleep for twenty years.

The legend of Hudson haunting the Hudson River valley was part of the region's folklore long before Irving's time. It is a curious legend for several reasons. At the time of his disappearance, Hudson was sailing for the English, not the Dutch, and not aboard the *Half Moon*. Furthermore, he was last seen in Hudson Bay, hundreds of miles north of the Hudson River and the Catskills. Despite the lapses in logic, Washington Irving could not resist a good ghost story.

Rip Van Winkle returns home after a twenty-year slumber following an encounter with the ghost of Henry Hudson and his crew in Washington Irving's classic short story.

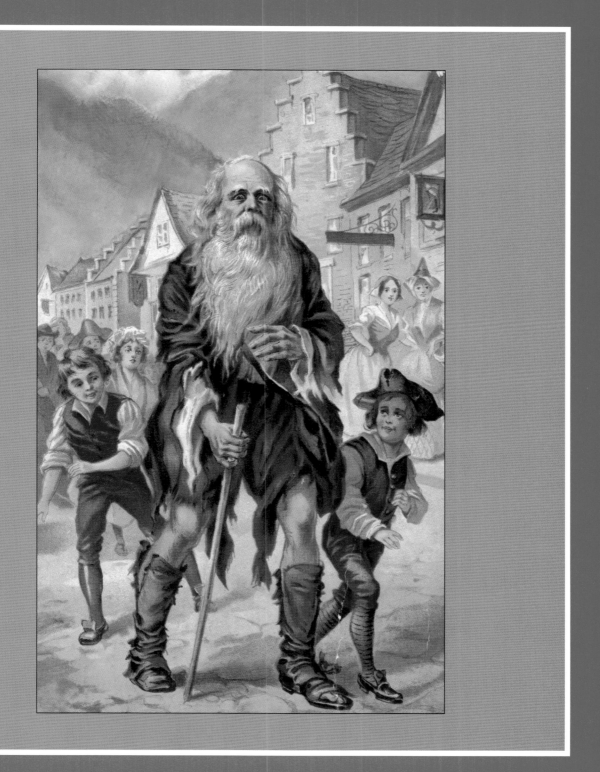

Afterword

In his own eyes, Henry Hudson might well have considered himself a failure. He never found a passage to Asia by traveling across the North Pole. Nor did he discover the Northwest Passage through North America. Five years after his last, ill-fated expedition, explorers Robert Bylot and William Baffin, sailing Hudson's ship the *Discovery*, proved beyond a doubt that Hudson Strait was not a passageway to the Pacific.

If one of the requirements for greatness is the ability to inspire others to reach a final goal despite obstacles, then Hudson arguably falls short.

And yet, he remains a great explorer. Although he never found the Northwest Passage, he still sailed farther north than any explorer before him. His discovery of the whales at Spitsbergen helped create the English whaling industry which flourished for several centuries. Though from a more environmentally conscious perspective it may be a dubious

ROBERT BYLOT – EXPLORER AND MUTINEER

Robert Bylot was a trained and respected navigator whose decision to join the mutiny onboard the *Discovery* should have caused his ruin. Yet Bylot's skills and knowledge of North America made him invaluable to England's trading companies.

After his return to England, he made four voyages to the Arctic and North America. On the last of these in 1617 Bylot explored a large bay north of Hudson Bay that bordered Greenland. Because of his involvement in the Hudson mutiny, Bylot was unable to name the bay and the large island to its south after himself. Instead, he named it for his pilot and navigator, William Baffin. Today they still bear the names Baffin Bay and Baffin Island.

Bylot returned to England after this final expedition, and nothing further is known of his life. Baffin was killed in the Persian Gulf in 1622 while serving in the British army.

Whalers remove strips of blubber or fat from a dead whale. The whaling industry owed much to Hudson's discovery of the huge mammals off the coast of Spitsbergen.

achievement, it was an economic advantage for England at a critical time of national growth.

Hudson's memorable voyage up the river that today bears his name opened up the region of present-day New York State to Dutch colonization. Dutchman Peter Minuit purchased Manhattan Island from the Indians only fifteen years after Hudson's expedition. The Dutch quickly settled much of the fertile Hudson River valley, and their New Netherlands was a thriving colony when the English seized control of it in 1664.

Hudson's exploration of Hudson Bay gave the English an important

KATHERINE HUDSON, "THAT TROUBLESOME WOMAN"

In her own way, Hudson's wife was as strong willed and determined as he was. Little is known about Katherine Hudson's life until her husband's disappearance in 1611. It was her persistence that finally convinced the East India Company to send out their first rescue mission to find her husband and son three years later. (Other ships had looked for them before this.) In any event, by then the rescuers were too late to be of any help to them.

Katherine then pressed the EIC to give her compensation for her loss, leading it to brand her as "that troublesome and impatient woman." Her impatience, however, paid off. The company made her their agent in Ahmadabad, India, where she purchased indigo, an important dye for clothing. The sale of the indigo in England made her a wealthy woman.

In her final years, Hudson lobbied to have a monument honoring her husband erected in London, but her dream was never realized. Katherine Hudson died in September 1624 at her London home, survived by her sons Richard and Oliver.

claim to the region. It also led to the establishment in 1670 of England's Hudson's Bay Company, one of the first and largest fur-trading companies in North America. The company's success gave England a foothold in Canada, which would eventually lead the English to drive out the French in 1763 and build their own Canadian empire.

Henry Hudson was a flawed hero, who was a far better explorer than leader. Yet his courage, perseverance, navigational skills, and determination helped to open up an uncharted continent when few were willing to brave the wilds of an unknown land.

Hudson's exploration of the Hudson River valley led to the area being colonized by the Dutch and later the English.

Henry Hudson
and His Times

about 1570   Hudson is born in London, England.

1587   John Davis discovers and explores the Furious Overfall in North America. Hudson is possibly a member of his crew.

1607   Hudson sails on his first voyage for the Muscovy Company to find a passage to the East by crossing the North Pole, but is driven back by ice.

1608   His second voyage takes him to Novaya Zemlya, north of Russia, but he again fails to find a passage to the East.

1609

April   Hudson sails for the Dutch on his third voyage to find a passage to the East, but changes his course for North America.

September–October

He explores the Hudson River as far north as present-day Albany, New York.

November–December

He returns to England and is accused of treason by King James I.

1610

April   Hudson leaves England on his fourth and final voyage and heads for North America.

June–August

Hudson reaches the Furious Overfall (Hudson Strait) and sails into Hudson Bay.

November

> He and his crew settle in for the winter in ice-covered James Bay.

1611

June 22 or 24

> Hudson's crew mutinies and puts him, his son, and several others adrift in a small boat. They are never seen again.

October

> The surviving mutineers reach London.

1616–1617

> Robert Bylot and William Baffin visit and explore Baffin Island and Baffin Bay, north of Hudson Bay.

1618   The four surviving mutineers are put on trial and found not guilty.

1624   The Dutch purchase Manhattan Island from the Indians and establish New Amsterdam (later called New York City).

1670   The Hudson's Bay Company, an English fur-trading company, is founded on the shores of Hudson Bay.

Further Research

Books

Edwards, Judith. *Henry Hudson and His Voyages of Exploration in World History.* Berkeley Heights, NJ: Enslow, 2002.

Kline, Trish. *Henry Hudson.* Vero Beach, FL: Rourke, 2003.

Mattern, Joanne. *The Travels of Henry Hudson.* Austin, TX: Steadwell Books, 2000.

Sherma, Josepha. *Henry Hudson: English Explorer of the Northwest Passage.* New York: Rosen, 2003.

Syme, Ronald. *Henry Hudson.* New York: Marshall Cavendish, 1991.

Weiner, Eric. *The Story of Henry Hudson, Master Explorer.* New York: Dell, 1991.

West, Tracey. *Voyage of the Half Moon.* New York: Silver Moon Press, 1993.

Web Sites

Ian Chadwick:

The Life & Voyages of Henry Hudson English Explorer & Navigator

http://www.ianchadwick.com/hudson

Who Was Henry Hudson Anyway and What Happened to Him?

Half Moon Press

http://www.hudsonriver.com/halfmoonpress/stories/hudson.htm

The Hudson River

http://www.hudsonriver.com

BIBLIOGRAPHY

Asimov, Isaac, and Elizabeth Kaplan. *Henry Hudson: Arctic Explorer and North American Adventurer.* Milwaukee: Gareth Stevens, 1991.

Gerson, Noel Bertram. *Passage to the West: The Great Voyages of Henry Hudson.* New York: J. Messner, 1968.

Goodman, Joan E. *Beyond the Sea of Ice: The Voyages of Henry Hudson.* New York: Mikaya Press, 1999.

Johnson, Donald S. *Charting the Sea of Darkness: The Four Voyages of Henry Hudson.* New York: Kodansha, 1995.

Manning, Ruth. *Henry Hudson.* Chicago: Heinemann Library, 2001.

Saffer, Barbara. *Henry Hudson: Ill-Fated Explorer of North America's Coast.* Broomall, PA: Chelsea House, 2002.

Santella, Andrew. *Henry Hudson.* New York: Franklin Watts, 2001.

Vail, Philip. *The Magnificent Adventures of Henry Hudson.* New York: Dodd, Mead, 1965.

Source Notes

Chapter 2:

p. 12   "an experienced seaman. . . ." Web site: Ian Chadwick. "Henry Hudson: The Life & Voyages of Henry Hudson English Explorer & Navigator," http://www.ianchadwick.com/hudson

Chapter 3:

p. 19   "very high land for the most part. . . ." Web site: Chadwick, http://www. ianchadwick.com/hudson

p. 23   "May God give us. . . ." Barbara Saffer, *Henry Hudson: Ill-Fated Explorer of North America's Coast*, p. 16.

Chapter 4:

p. 26   "She was close to the ship's side. . . ." Joan E. Goodman, *Beyond the Sea of Ice: The Voyages of Henry Hudson*, p. 15.

p. 31   "sunk into the lowest depths. . . ." Web site: Chadwick, http://www. ianchadwick.com/hudson

Chapter 5:

pp. 33, 36 "by the north around the north side of Nova Zembla." Goodman, p. 19.

p. 36 "I hope that these square-faced men know the sea. . . ." Web site: Chadwick, http://www.ianchadwick.com/hudson

Chapter 6:

p. 42   "the finest for cultivation. . . ." Isaac Asimov and Elizabeth Kaplan, *Henry Hudson: Arctic Explorer and North American Adventurer*, p. 30.

p. 43   "killed . . . and skinned . . . in great haste." Web site: Chadwick, http:// www.ianchadwick.com/hudson

Source Notes

Chapter 7:

p. 45   "voyaging to the detriment. . . ." Web site: Chadwick, http://www.ianchadwick.com/hudson

Chapter 8:

p. 52   "the mountaynes of ice" Web site: Chadwick, http://www.ianchadwick.com/hudson

p. 58   "The house was finally made. . . ." Goodman, p. 38.

p. 58   "We went . . . in search of anything. . . ." Saffer, p. 48.

Afterword:

p. 71   "that troublesome and impatient woman." Web site: Chadwick, http://www.ianchadwick.com/hudson

INDEX

Page numbers in **boldface** are illustrations.

Index